# MODERN FOG

# CHRIS EMERY

# MODERN FOG

2024

Published by Arc Publications,
Nanholme Mill, Shaw Wood Road
Todmorden OL14 6DA, UK
www.arcpublications.co.uk

978 1911469 54 4 (pbk)
978 1911469 73 5 (ebk)

Design by Tony Ward
Printed in Great Britain by
TJ Books, Padstow, Cornwall

Cover image: © CSA-Printstock / Getty Images

**Arc Publications UK and Ireland Series:**
**Series Editor: Tony Ward**

*for Elspeth*
(1947–2022)


Deep calls to deep
at the roar of your waterfalls;
all your breakers and your waves
have gone over me.

PSALM 42:7

# CONTENTS

## ROOMS

Inside the sweet and charmless one, the filthy one,
the room with flies or night wasps singing far too high.
Shutterless and bleached and all-too-ready-rooms,
the gassy room, fitted out with pique and sorrow,
the one cascading with cries and fags and sweet wine –
or sheltering nothing but canker and steel dusk.
The small one, adhered to in that long interior absence.
The large one, teak-filled, leaking news of Edwardian deaths.
The creaking one where someone close, closer
and terrible, is taking steps, when the steps reached you.

The one that burning afternoon, filled with dust
lit-up below a silent ceiling fan where laughter
reached in and up before the midday call to prayer.
The one you absconded from by the green night shop,
seeing triple on a bad trip, your nose ceaselessly bleeding.
The one you cannot see, being born amid the tall sparks.
The one you come to see unhoused, with thin stars
or evening traffic, filled with faces you almost knew.
A final bed, the last of hope, but everything inclement
withering fast on a lane of mad white flowers.

## THE PATH

All the no-shows picking their way
through whin and leaf mould along the path,
with England's wild attendance
flinging or fleeing, will not remind.

And all that hot wheat falling
and chalk beds, the clay beds, sinking
through each gold afternoon,
those wrapped inside rowan
elsewhere beside dirt paths alone,
bursting and feeding,
the air full of tares in a grinding wake,
shielding their mouths,
where I will ask you to stop
among it all,
to stand and see beyond motionless blackthorn
the sweet chestnuts sweeping our silent blue,
the far pale hills, a single jay,
a single buzzard blithely turning where
I shall ask you to forget this white hour
and climb with me to the king oak.

Somehow we will reach it, planting a quarterstaff
to recognise a new path, screeds plain, screeds poor,
below things seen and expendable
and you can take my hand and stand there, panting.
I have led you here through all possible music
for something we cannot wholly know
and you will pull up my hand and kiss it
and carefully we walk on.

## THE DAY STORM

Stopping here in the deer scrub
where bramblings panic,
you come to notice
low chaotic thickets, silent
spattered ridges cut through
with twists of blackthorn
and blackberry and small nettle
yielding nothing in the mess.

And above it all, transported
from yesterday's once-in-a-century wind
a score of tall lives are clarified:
red pines, oaks and beeches gashed
in angled embraces, splintered
with heavy breaks, hanging on
to make sense of it all
as the sap runs out.

# STAGS

*As a deer pants for flowing streams,*
*so pants my soul for you...*

Psalm 42:1

When you see that they have passed like fire dreams
you wake to, you'll know they have run through
what's forsaken. You can't remember how
each was elegant, bronze, and silent

where now the hawthorn is readjusting,
waving briefly, having stored such regal frames.
All that remains is absence in sycamore
shoots, alder and ash and rhododendron

that seem urgent now. They've gone, and the dogs
are astounded at the edge of what's never
fully grasped: nothing to chase into mould
and stasis below the cold fitting pines,

yet still, inside your eyes, the chestnut haunches
of the broken gods you wish to see here
are this store of grace and loss for you.
It is the last religion in these woods.

## THE VISIT

All the grandmothers in the world
are gathered beneath a willow,
its green drapes are filled with black fly.
They are wearing Linton dresses,
garters, aprons, slippers and brooches,
and they talk about sheep or sewing.

They all loudly agree everything is dying,
even Edna with her tenacious pig,
everyone is dying or ill or drunk,
and men stink. It is three o'clock, children
begin to squirm from red shadows
to burn like lights in the park.

The grandmothers fall silent, watching.
Some begin to cry at the bright scene
while the children roll their eyes,
wander by the willow, hot with life.
In far hills darkened by diesel, men
prepare tanks for one final visit.

## VISITING HOURS

I remember what we all remember:
the smart fish of her hands slapping
the froth on the flour board

and her brow deep and lamentable
above tired dough,
deep and lamentable. And then

amber was it, or jet, or filigree silver:
a blister in the drawer that stuck and unstuck.
The charms without a bracelet.

The bracelet without charms.
A cough at the grey window, nets drawn,
naturally enough on the day,

keeping watch in her stone-silent, cream
and gunmetal grey parlour;
the risk that kept the birdcage shut.

And the phantom edge, the solemn cut
indifference has, piled with last week's papers
beside a white jug, a bare mantelpiece,

the crochet drooped over
a wild brocade chair, worn through,
and the tiniest infant charm buried in it.

Something lost and lost again tied to an
irretrievable anchor, her steadfastness
watching you play, her finger raised.

## THE BITTERN

*for Richard Lambert*


We moored at How Hill in loose light
and bird song. Two marsh harriers
bowled up their thermal. One heron
made its pikestaff in the sedge wall.

Evening leaked west as, one by one,
some human singers let their song
drift down to fill the field and staithe,
the big house concert over now.

Did they step out to hear the geese
weave their sorrows and silhouettes?
Settled then, the humans and birds,
when a new sound underpinned us

like a bottle neck when blown like this,
a bass *whoomph*, or far off fog horn
unplaced, lost beneath things, like love,
repeating through the night for us.

# CROMER

Come with me to Cromer Ridge,
I have 430,000 reasons to make you rich:
the cogs of the moraine
and sewing wheels of sharp terns, just watch

that lone muntjac swim, who knew,
under a peach and butter sky,
as the sun learns its lines from the beach's
cobbled scabs and tatters and everything is new

for you, and look again, the muntjac
is staggering free from the fan white surf now
and the first people have arrived
to spear the light loaned to them, and they are staggered.

You can push through your hard breath
into the decadent loyal plush of landslips
and mudflows that twist the cliff face here,
over the mad bone hoard and this far east

face north in the arc of nothing whole,
the broken feast that barks and screeches,
farther and farther, and leaves you undone,
burning under a partial moon and this lifting sun.

## THE BUZZARD

Heat enough to bring forgotten adders out.
Old gorse swaddled in pink dodder.
It is a churchless afternoon. One shout
to a lost dog, one to a lost deer
on this acid grassland hill
we climb, until
we burn and snort at the summit,
spying on small drives and breeding waves.
Above us, in its immaculate empire,
a bird whisks up and saves
its eyes for the militant hour.
Has its cry gone wrong?
Dying without song
we hope to crave what this bird craves.

It might be the Roman road beyond Burnt Lane,
where bats occupy a partial disused bunker
beyond the corporation park, rusted goal posts
and fossilised rides above a perished rubber mesh,
where one dog barks its way into the kingdom.
Or a Viking lane that circumvents abnormal
ancient beeches, whitethorn in ratty spurts,
where you meet the twilight walkers circling –
taking their bad hips out to avoid
lonely suppers in the Saracen's Head.
Or that unclear path, stone clumped, webby,
beside mid-century prefabs, whose wired gardens
are punctuated with prams and trikes
and trampolines no one uses. You wonder
if the path is real this close to the fences.
Or a Puritan lane in witless sunshine that skirts
the big house and cottages then skulks by
something like an orchard, over thyme fields
and rhubarb, sloping to St Winifred's, its dry mud
rutted enough to make each journey resolute.

# PENTECOST

Small snatch of air, sole white arc,
crisp handclap, then ritual landing.
All followed by cosseting and fuss
at the stoop. The laughable dance
with lots of nodding and wittering
before the tricky hop up
to the dovecote, its painted chassis
cut with arches.

The wind is picking up. It weaves
its sweet chill along the lane.
Birches and hydrangeas bustle and bend
in a fast descent of shadows.
What can we say? Our ears fill
with town music watching the show.
Now it's time to go in, to stir the grates,
to light all the fires.

# THE BAY

A sort of dislodged washed-out bay
we fell into after hours of hill torture.
No terns or boats, no breeze to speak of,
but laces of white water moving fast and,
farther off, the shattered hem of a ness.
Spilled before it, a wide green stony spread
and the afterthought of winter crofting:
salt white walls, salt white doors, copper roofs,
turf-piled yards and sweet tails of smoke.

Most things will end, the mind in time,
work and teeth and knees and hips, but there
among the still weather and homesteads
all the short-lived shadows you could know
hold their ounce of love before the land runs out.

# EDGEWORLDS

Thin rain at the storm edge
sweeping inshore towards grey
relinquished emplacements
where, below, rapacious fish waste
never hears its buried river.
New 4×4s line the flint pocked
esplanade as each cream tide subsides
from remedial concrete plateaux
and all our four o'clock predicaments
undo in derelict rooms
where no eyes dream of hired gold.
Life spreads out its bedspread
in the sad afternoon and
we find solace or affection
or pretence of it in a hall full of
palatial minor trimmings
as dust falls on a radiogram
and out beyond worming sea fret
we see, forever shaded, sprawling north,
something finger the ratty beach
under grey parallel acts
of sky and earth – and deeper still
that globe twist or star funk
while organ music flares up here
for the coach tour at six.
It must be time for foxtrots
as those gussied up wait for takers,
then soft tambourines later.
Still, outside more long rain
works its wild skirts through
memories like a knife. Soon,
detergent in blue corridors

releases memories of dinner
and the gravy-coloured craquelure
of banisters in this flaky
hotel, cascades in silent curlicues
towards a one-armed porter
eating chips, watching reruns
on the last available television.

## THE NOVEL

The last, green-tiled cinema
and slave-financed squares with dogs.
One cherry-coloured Gothic
tower leaking minor debts
across this gloss paint kerb-spill
displaying size eight boot prints
ending here.

Wild Euclidean allure:
deep warehouse nights, pawn shops, bars,
a canal filled with condoms,
and lost Victoriana
cracking under viaducts.
We have these cash free comforts
to hurt us.

Then I wanted you to walk
through a small triumph of pills
into the city harbour,
displaced from my tears, my teeth,
dragging all our music out,
finding dry workaday truths
to write about and this novel
I die in.

## THE WALL PAINTINGS

*St Andrew, Wickhampton*


The thunk of a latch and then your eyes adjust.
Is it oxide in the paint that knows the longueurs
of this church? Outside, trees sort their coral shadows.
Inside, we stall with love below a pictured hare.

'And there they are,' I say, pointing to what's clear.
'Just the same,' you whisper, then cough in milky light.
The nave fills with a sound of crop winds
and a backlog of dreams and lost messages.

Someday, we'll revisit the quick and the dead,
adherents of the what-comes-next:
'*As you are, we were; as we are, you will be.*'
all the days fail finally with such reclaims in life.

## THE ELDERS

*i.m. Adam Zagajewski*

The old dogs lying in spring sun
collecting new shadows for us.

Nothing was the same after the revolution
for we wore new chains.

Now each steps over
the wild oak limbs where they lie

broken with new life.

## A CHILDHOOD IN WINTER

Who can know the way – the sky one furnace
near the drum of the town? All that's damp is
stowed on the road down, and soon, lit-up drops
shaking and shaking on the ferns. A new
mist where the roe deer chewing berries stop
inside the hunger of it all. The few
facts we find in a separating love.
We are blank rags of winter and the proof,
if proof were needed, is for our sake
the hours die. Soon we shoulder white daybreak.
Nothing gives. Ten rooks explain a birch copse.
We stagger down towards the framing crops.
Tiny frozen neighbours in a childhood
that will widow us, lost and found, for good.

## CONDORS

We practise making condor shadows next,
working the yard, squawking and hollering
as flies make a gauze in the porch light.

The dreamy sky is yellow, then russet under
an octave of stars. If you look past the Clancys' place
you can see bunkers and palms and mountains

pass into the night's cauldron. No one knows
how to start things in this place. I ask you if you
understand the marriage of things when it gets dark,

you say the world belongs to itself for sure.
Anyhow, we stop to watch the phantom sun hang
over the freeway. You can be anything here.

## AFTERWARDS

Four days after my death
I begin to itch.
Is it normal?
Loneliness not abating.
I imagined the afterlife
crowded with corpses,
a chatty throng moving
along twilight
pastureland, far pink mountains,
fountains where the dogs pause
in their urgent shadows.

Is everyone's death like this?
After the bizarre cupboard
company of the forelife,
to come to this place in Denver.

So many stories and films
point towards those hunkered lingering
in hinterlands, managing to interfere
with loved ones and enemies.

The buildings and landscapes all changed,
there are no humans,
no animals at all. When I wake
my adjectives perish with the pale blond sun.

I imagine the creaking trees,
sallow horses, shrieking birds, but nothing comes.
No sound. I hear my thoughts.
I imagine the sounds of the world
each time I wake and I realise

increasingly petulant
that the wild sounds are gone.
There is no point talking
in this moon mirror life.

All the forgettable rage of the world:
its burning trees, its soaking fields,
mud ridges that loped with bodies once.
Tarpaulins in squalid rain
before the torrent bit through
and spilled the separately lifeless into
their beige wasting lake.

## HIGH FOOTAGE

High, soot-green ghost plunge, and then this:
an outreach of knocking autumn
on some stakeless shore. Riverless.
Attendanceless. Imagine us
among the clacking absences
with so much shale and long sea dreck
in dismal contour lines the sea
has wrung from burned islands. Out here
north is nothing. And yet the wind
fans an ankle of moon in cheap
cirrus stretches – that sudden light-
bloat, its halo pouring by clouds
where each threadless local mind tunes
scratchy radios for union
on this fog-taunted edge and sighs
into a life made less in parts
by the land's dying shoulders. Unst,
seeping in blue black waves, whose love
among the wreckage somehow shaved
back into this decent vacant
terrace, lightless on the scrap ridge?
The gardens tipping vertically
with scabby vestiges, pipework,
islands of dead crockery caught
in the chalk retreats easing through
such poor thin days. And on the headland,
beside the feather white breakers,
a dozen bonxies trade life wares
in smooth wet ridges the weather makes.
An abundant unlit ruin
some of us can find solace in,
life's small achievements left sodden
in a night's wild cemeteries.

## THE SNAKE

No one told him he could fly at night,
that the cellar bars were simply chocolate,
the locks unread books.

No one told him he could make his deep mother
from apple pips and spider legs
in the latrine.

No one read bedtime stories for the warm earth
with its bolted tunnel was a sleeping
fizzing snake he lived in,

whose pricks of seminary lights hung along
its throat were stars. He had crashed to earth in a chariot
made of sacks.

Years later, blinking at the sheriff, he witnessed
the birth of his father, and two tunes,
blue and white, like his own skin.

## THE SADNESS OF RADIO

Working through peach bathrooms
it lets us whine about boys.
All skin and bone
and moodless margarine,
below each monocled moon
the cold news thaws.

Watch them push a half-million
gas night roasts
through Sunday like a laxative.
We're taking pets from town to town,
driving through thunderstorms
in a garbage countdown
to the metal noon.

Crowds gather in footless forests for sex
beside towns of see-through cats and car parks,
it provides a form of discipline for men.
And foxes lift their mouths
to lemon dials, pressing to visit
a lifetime of dead ears.
Someone absolutely sings.

Inside such wafer-thin miracles
a million women gather to ignore the violet rooms
while boys officiate through hours like cigarettes.
And the wallpaper shrivels, the wax melts
and tonnes of chiffon
and taffeta expire with deluxe anniversaries.
Such listless azure forever
scraping teeth
with wasted sunbeams.

## AT ST HELEN'S, RANWORTH

I

At first
small redactions
of pale sun shear the cold
nave of O so many hard years,
and find some shame in me, some shame
that has no potted shadows
and will not cause a misstep or fall.
Do I notice the present stone mind,
its slight shift in entering? No.
Something certain covets
certain pickings that here
skew awe for doubt. Insisting on
blindness for erstwhile truth, that lies
inside the knocking stations
you step through, like a hart
in its grey monotony. But no.
The mildew and mint air saps
with that scintillating pressure,
keeping your entire human score.
Imagine the immanence of God's lens,
that lens drawing in the loving iris
winding down new angels
on through the wingèd column
the stiff throat, heart enamel, too,
and into our smallest life. Watching,
veering though the tight soul,
to witness cold demotions of love.
His loving hands, the washing
hands, that would later bleed
taking up each soiled foot.

Up and up,
I climbed,
threading the stone gullet,
a fantail of stone above me, whorling.
The central simple pillar just
one hand's width that I pushed away,
smooth and cold, then this body's
width of air, the chary steps,
the outer wall of gritty render
paler than the cleated stones
set in to it. I was the dark itself
climbing, chafing against
what narrowed, startled by
angular light that cut through
staggered little windows, showing
silent trees. And held tightly
to what? My hard years feeding,
dear God, the hold ups and hold outs,
twisting with my heaviest breaths
as I stepped on, laughing
blindly that it should end. And then
I heard a sudden higher noise
clarifying in the spiral case
and froze, worried naturally, unable
to turn back and squinting
to see whose pale feet descended
from the stain above. I moved
into a single inset door frame,
and listened, hunting the dark
for whatever would come.

III

A steel ladder
at a sudden angle,
the umber rungs glinting and
clammy as I gripped it. Rising,
it juddered like a bass note would
in the chest wall, a wound of air
I hung out over, pausing to see
the bell wheelhouse, its
louvred Norman windows,
that showed nothing.
Last year, I came and would not
climb, my mind could not climb
this dim winding corpus and I
watched you all rise in its throat.
Here in the tampered space
I move through the tower now,
reaching for its tiny wooden
plateau, six feet under the sun,
where the second ladder leans,
its silty wooden slats tensing
by a black trap door. Every word
is trapped within. The life
at its hinge. Something you sheath
for a small and tender thing,
the toil I would push back into
abashed under the zenith.
Something shifted, I hurried up
into golden wanton bluster –
all around the waters shivered
and I listed on my mast.

IV

                    Quaint,
              unattainable,
viridian estates, all nestled in
beside the visceral waters.
The wind drubbed weathervane
and Brother Pacificus with his dog
bailing and spinning his rusty coracle,
journeying rivers from St Benet's,
restoring what was ruined.
Do you remember our time there?
Walking to the winter charcoal bench,
islanded, hearing its piping chants
above speedwell and thyme.
Christ in his field of absences,
the lost afternoon declined into
unnatural abundance. Still, here below
St Helen's our bright staithe knocks
its white boats now, high far birds
wheel their arcs, making separate
ascents into shocking cerulean.
I begin my descent, but stop
to let some newcomers raise
their arms and anoraks through
the roof. We stand together, wall-eyed
in spreading weather and then
I grope towards the small mouth
and step in backwards, sending
back my false smile, feeling the rungs
at my feet, no mythic cord or thread,
making my descent.

V

   You learn
  what to leave,
yet I had come here with you.
Should I but hear the facts
peering into seams that held
each star field abutted to,
the regular universe we know we know.
How vague the mustered fragments,
pitted names smaller and yet
smaller, each bending through
our customary origin. But here
I lean in to a governing mystery,
to see the teal, the plum and gold,
the tapped, petal-dotted panels
in trefoiled inset oblongs
bearing the apostles. And I see
perfect feet, the telling symbols,
combined indifferent glances,
steering my eyes down, where someone
so tenderly and hemmed with brushes
has painted each perfect finger,
the clean attentive hands,
yellow hair tugged back under halos
and audacious beards and lustrous
gold cassocks. I marvel how
it has survived its own cause
and downfall to reach us, the story that
holds the story, the matter of it
that reaches us from a common tree,
a thriving binding root.

Sure, no one
is made certain.
I need you outstretched
wild in the other land.
I listen and you move in.
I am infested yet you come.
Our brisket burning century
neither confessing or pleading,
our deep needs not buttressed
with shriving. I look on those here,
so button bright inside their frames.
Reaching beyond the lavish trellis,
not to solve the negative chancel
but to house us. To hold
what we are of the church,
to be fabric and pane, image
and counterimage in
the bloody beck and call. They had
doubted easily the vision thing
that held us wretched, writhing
through the parish to land
before the foreign furniture
so fierce with God. It must burn
and burn it did. Everyone
lit with the destroying angel
while the worlds fell, the roods
smashed, the Saints haphazardly buried
by carpenters and priests, to be
lifted later from each needful pit
into what we could know.

                    A simple
                word that salves.
Who would choose no inner life?
We strained the livid marsh, old
reed beds filled with cowbane,
hemp agrimony, lilting tainted
oaks so torn and ivy bound
it is impossible to own the route.
Fen orchids spreading through
an amber-lit carr woodland that
sings each evening. O the song
above silver forging wet woods
where a moon corrugates the sky
with lit up cirrus and bitter stars.
All those owl-deepened edges
you know are closing in,
to leave you with night perfume,
to fill your head with
wild astringent. Vespers
then compline. At midnight,
I rise to praise you and the chilly
waters underglaze
the frozen boat. Who knew
we would dent the River Bure
to be back here, to stutter through,
to see the heron-sorted sedge
and verge on what came in
among us, to take us through reeds,
to speak without a mouth
about the tiniest of chambers.

> Spare arrivals,
> no departures,
all that wetland to and fro made flat,
the silent River Ant drifting through
a world all emerald and silver,
yet not banal. We puttered through
lost cranes and kingfishers –
Neatishead to Irstead, low tunes,
slow clawed banks of black earth.
Then How Hill to St Benet's,
all sibilance and reticence as
tiny breakers met the mud flanks.
No sycamores or oaks to flood
the air. And then we landed.
What was it we should bring?
A lung of smoke, backstops
of skittering day birds,
all that skims and darts, plush
air brimming with cold consolation?
You lifted me and looked out,
taking the binoculars to search
and search for something
no one can see. The fall away
of garments like a sheet of sin.
Something brooding and territorial
lost within, and the wild arms
reaching across damp empty acres
to meet us, winding in the ropes,
getting the knots wrong as
the prow slowly drifted out.

We keep
coming back.
What can we teach ourselves
in the seminary waterways?
All those tie ups and stern kicks,
how to feed the early jazzy ducks,
or lessons in emptiness. Here
now, Malthouse Broad fakes its
tourists – the chintzy shops
of bird scarves and bird cards
and bird littoral stationery –
we hover to pick and stare, abandoned
before taking the jaunty trek
back to St Helen's. The green lane
beyond a fenced off glister of boats,
tacking, ribald sunlight breaking in
weekly addenda of hedging,
then we see your lavish tower
sorting some prince of earth
rehousing something clustered
to be here. Not a savage change
or bitter culmination of the facts,
six hundred years of stone
that break upon the modern fog.
Our inside eyes soon set on feathered
St Michael, dragon slayer, patron
of mariners, the dull sword slung
out over what was presaged,
a world we could come to know.
Have come to now.

X

              Of course,
              soft rowbacks
will settle in, elsewhere
the teeth and lips of these tidal ridges
become just ours in hard sleep,
we jostle for mooring. Adrift.
Agog at the nearly true, the neat finish,
the island wheat beaten flat
with what we wanted to be true.
Each of us unreeved,
our devil-may-care, scoffing
suitabilities that don't rear so much
as bloat. Rotting silent beeches,
stagnant liverwort and lichen.
All it takes to be the ghost here
missing low registers,
the doubt we need to live
brushed aside as if all of us were waste.
We cannot know, and cannot yield.
Hushed with what is tauntingly tribal,
we shrink from old sedge to the new.
But the story of these twelve
taking the screaming heat of the air
for a new measure, speaking
wildly over the din of the room,
we cannot endarken it
haltered for the pure ride out.
The mystery is its abatement:
the staff, the spear, the sword
the book, the fuller's staff, the boat.

I want
to give you this
in a frame of tight Tudor roses –
a baize green day we bend in to,
to see inside the scalloped frame,
the geometric lozenged floor,
one entrance to the absolute.
All that typical lustre
you know the crowds would see
gathered in not reading
but seeing between fingers
pattern and foment,
the clear mind, the clean skin.
Everything that lasts within.
After lost days in the boat,
I laugh at all this giddying freshness.
Yet that's not it, it's this:
I want to stitch my dark
to yours inside a river ritual.
Something the walls may
register above the dry piscina there
a thousand years from now.
Something I will not understand
but still impart. A small thing
nesting resolute duties
and all those interstices
to fill the fully human.
That we can submit to
like a clear day over which
wild geese congregate.

I tease
free the last knot,
the engine ticks, the stern drops
and the dawn waters thicken.
We move off for Horning,
for Salhouse and Wroxham.
Dark birds tip the cabled sky. Cabled waters
fatten and twist beneath
spreads of chestnut and alder.
What we leave, we shall bring;
common courtesies of spring.
All that presides over the river
lies inside each other now, the bustle
yields between otters and grebes –
deep calls to deep and we suspire.
Behind us, Ranworth sheds
its gold deliveries, common terns
pierce the cloud-line, but we drift on
lavishly desacralised,
bidding all well for the need
of each river hour, turning and turning,
missing the proper steering aim
before finding a fresh line.
I'm glaring at blue birch scrub
that bears no name, its unfenced
mad mosaic subsiding to glottal life.
Back there, inside the vestigial,
apostles of the inundation
stand neatly pinned in oak,
thin light knits, then spreads.

## WHALSAY

All I remember is that drip pour of land
and the mainland settled in a laminate sea

and loose afternoon as deep as your hair
and all that could be gripped was free

on a crisp green field – the warmth of your ribs,
the ship of our breath, when the sky burned mauve

and citrine and russet over Lunning or Lunna
with the dark birds crying, 'Love her in Skaw.'

And the North Sea answered and pinned us there
with a ring for the moon and a ring for our hearts.

## COME DANCING

When you hitch up your braided dress
to mark a corn year and follow a tune
in old light across town,
below wet hills and town soot
and by the dogs of the town,
let our sweet mothers know
you will come dancing.

And as you whirl by crossroads
and fields of beets and peas
they will come to watch
and draw you on to conifers,
safe at the half-lit ridge.
You'll see that every woman
steps through the shape of Danu.

## THE MEMORY BOX

Put back the large plate shots, tin types
all cream and sienna craquelure
and put back the dubious Polaroid
with its cyan veneer. Put back
the deckle-edged monochrome snaps
and the impossible fragile thumbnails, too.
Put back all the views of car-less lanes,
pale smocks and strap sandals, and puffed vintage cloud,
the unremembered incoherent garden with its
lavish, brutal rhododendrons groping
someone, hidden, blurred, twisting
out of frame.

Then fold the tea-stained tissue back,
that Edith ripped in '67, arguing with Albert
or Edward over matins and cake;
when the Blackpool band played something
quite unusual on the radio but no one
listened. And once they are all imposed and ordered,
squirm your hands over the piles
to smooth down its patchwork,
levelling out the paper residue of pals and foes
we shall eventually burn, discard or
sell on a trestle table in the Jubilee Hall
no one visits now.

And then take the satin lid with its tiny
purple regal hem and push it slowly down
on the box that softly resists
and makes an incontrovertible hiss
like this, the very sound our past makes
with its hair cream and antimacassars.

The sound of someone sucking false teeth
at an extravagant expensive fabric, the sound
of the quince-flavoured breath of someone
about to begin their last errand on earth.
Now lift the box to smell our loneliest ever island,
place it in the drawer and shut it tight.

## THE STYLIST

*for George*


Through my chocolate-tinted door they come
wrapped in tiny worries: medication, rent and losses,
grandkids sifted through city parks,
their parents working on a rota. They tell me of
holidays with friends, a Baltic cruise filled
with scores of meals and city harbours long forgotten.

Some arrive surprised with glue-faced middle age
to stare at someone else's mop, disguised in choppy styles
and colours dragged from 1983. They want to know
what has become of every relegated dream.

And there and then, I cut them free and watch
their smiles return with almost mystery, the locks
falling in heaps in what could be contrition.
I see their hair surround them in a halo on the floor.

Perhaps I am their priest, I care for them so much.
I pull away the mirror and twist myself around them
to sterilise the scissors. Jean-Paul brushes down
and takes a card. And then I wave them off
for another month of something like new life,
my blow-dried, modernised, fresh-cut souls.

## THE MERGER

Then it passed between us
in the high room, oak shutters parted,
the two of us listening to the sobriquets
of passers-by and traders yelling high deceits –
the scouring market fading,
the heat a dream, the dream so hot
we formed a simple absence of ourselves
in the reckless afternoon.

It was a leaf of death we held, a grief of sorts,
the shame-need story of this decaying city
where we merged into each other,
soft as the blue shade in a cool piazza
where that hidden singer left his arias
hanging over the Angelus bell.

## MR BARDAKÇI

The last song on this street
is praying for light,
where Mr Bardakçı shifts
trays of mangoes and galangal
and sweet dandy lettuce –
he bends, coughs, lights a cigarillo
and hoicks up his tousers
(left side, then right),
and hears the kemençe.
All those crazy fattening years,
the damn years, riding this song
to the end of the world.

## DAY FOX

He had walked through Aylmerton to rest
and lie in thin December sun uncrushed
not timid but perfect there: his dream words
fished out beside an untrimmed singing verge.
On our first drive, he looked living amber
lying on lurid green moss all afternoon,
the way a boy lies spent in a dark field
unaware of linnets and nuthatches,
seeing only thin cirrus turning like milt
in clear water, the day ageing and running.

The next time we saw him, he'd gathered in weather
respectably dozing as dry weak hours
moved their clocks around him
with fresh silt driven in by the Felbrigg traffic,
dulling the understory tableaux,
where he had stayed his gorgeous ginger.

And then I lost sight of him, and wondered,
weeks later, if rooks had come and picked at him?
The day drives grew colder now, the fields tore
their wounds free and the hill storms
rushed in with high seas and moon sharp cold.

But then I noticed him today, unemployed
beside the chrome green residuum,
his pelt was coal tar black and slicked back
on the tiny lump of him, rain polished
and wasting but not burst or ripped gaudily
into dinner. He was pathetically shiny
and under-featured in the wet waste where
it seemed cruel nothing had feasted on him.

He was slowly withdrawing from us
nothing to clear the debris of him, the world
relaxed into him with all its fiery prayers.

## THE FROST WIFE

She will come on a horned moon night
with her fire sleigh singing,
with her dress of thorns and coal black eyes
she'll come ringing.

Killing foxes, working stoats across the hearsay snows,
knocking all your black horse cares
across fields where she scares
dead burrows.

You may see her on the river-stones carrying a knife
she'll peep into your eyes
to squeeze some kisses or goodbyes,
the frost wife.

## THE VISAGE

Watching drubbing water in a braid,
the sink slugging froth and swill,
you spot, askance, a punnet-headed you,
steam-enhanced, open mouthed,

picking at some teeth. Your hand
moves automatic through a pelmet fringe,
and what takes shape in sudden swipes
is excelsior years of frowning.

Standing at a double distance
there you are again – unknown, untrue –
a choreography of features in which
some idea dies, then fades from view.

## HARES

The crush fall of it all hedged in,
endings ended. Each seed glut poured
diesel- and barley-scented clouds

past each combine. Who came nightly
saw our crisp terraces lit-up
where your feet would crunch tomorrow's

stem white ardour dead. We waited.
Nothing could stop them dancing now.
Each evening, the retinal blue field

would suddenly flare up with them,
all ears and legs and black speed bursts
that kept to the spindled edges.

Something of their god stares under
tawdry rooks and uptakes of moon,
the swallow choirs and loose moorings

made them seem wilder and errant,
bringers of love or war or grief –
who knew their running-scared purpose?

Next season, when roads buckled dry,
hedges revealed their overcoats,
carcasses strewn in the blackthorn.

## LAURIE

Do not wait for me. Observe the seals.
Bring vodka to the sea cemetery there.
When the lapwings call, and the ghost light fails,
move between tall stones to see me
and the red ends of the Earth.

Sleep on the ticking shore and dream
of oars and nets and pitch and song.
Imagine moonlight paths on salt acres
and on those acres, birds and buoys.
At midnight, whistle. I will come.

Do not wait for me by grey town turrets
or soft currents or the silent stags and does
that come licking salt from night stones.
Ride the estuary east for the tongue of the dawn
and whistle, Laurie, whistle.

# HERITAGE

I don't know that Pat's fat bay is stamping out
the last misery of the year
as fog spills through grey Roscommon.
The pigs are out and the hens are out, yet
the candles are not lit by the two-foot coffin that sits
above McGeary, the pup on an oil cloth, whining.
And whomever sits and shakes below tinware
sees only the half-dark cupboard
with its three-slat door and latch.

It's no one's job to be here sober and in that pantry
in a small webbed space by a tan pint jug
are her smooth, green, tight-bowed shoes
from Knocknashee, worn once and danced in,
with heels like twelve-penny nails,
that travel on yet through a hundred years
when the food runs out, when the cold sets in,
and the child so long ago bleached out
waves through a soot cloud and is gone.

## L'affaire de l'art

And when I leased you all the things I knew
we made a bitter temple. The difference in our love spooled out
on dusty winter parquet. Lavish with risk, we ruled our bed.
'No kiss can be true enough,' you said, and I couldn't deviate,
trafficked each evening to be killed in you.

Our stories stripped in months of claggy absinthe.
The government of my hours knocked back,
staring at each maquette fried stiff inside its clock of limbs,
the easel flayed with time and yet our sun-bare god had turned
to spread new lies into each other. You were not proved,

I was not spent. Each breakfast was a meal of thorns.
I cried, 'I shall be wasted now,' you hissed that love was never free.
We set its price and monstered all we touched
in one more week of burning summer ink, its heat-fall of limbs.
We poured out all our bleach, or something very like it,
into what would be the very end, the very start of work.

## VOWS IN DORSET

I know you are there among limp irises,
plateaux of cigar smoke, sifting diner talk
that sings over this planned marriage.
I can cope with thin dog absence listening
to the idea of you, knowing you move like a crane
through a pearls and chiffon trail
towards the cold garden. And if I turn to watch
George rise and sniff through his funny story
of a meal in dismal Sherbourne in 1922,
or your mother's zeal for trout, no one laughs.
Yet now the rains begin, and willows draw closer
to swimming windows that hold you in their frame
where I shall never belong to you forever.

## ONE DRIVE IN WINTER

How far and why anyone would bother?
Where our satnav phased out and ran clear.
The petrol light flicked on. The road ahead
fringed with sycamore trees that then faded.
The lane tipped out beside dumped farm metal
and plucked fields. We killed the engine. It all
seemed fine, so fine, before the rain weakly
snaked over that maroon and lemon sky.

Well, if you think of it, that low burst world,
our maps spread out, the car cooling, us curled
over the old seats, I want you to know
I would drive there again, the same, just so,
to understand your low breath in the frost,
to make of it what we can, to laugh there,
to solemnise the marginal and lost,
to hold you close, to hear the inland shore.

## THE SEAL

*for Moniza Alvi*


We almost missed you in the Bure,
boulder-headed, as the river
bent towards Acle. There you were
all half-term nonchalance, fishing,
and we were shocked how far you'd come
to blink and watch our boat purling
through the big afternoon. We smiled
and then you were gone. River god,
sleek night bones, your soaked trunk twisting
through ochre waters, so special
and remote and even-handed,
taking what you wanted of bream
or perch or roach. That night, I dreamed
you drew through the shining mud
and raised yourself among low trees,
your dowsing coat still sleek and wet,
stepping out with that whiskered smile
and the fleurs-de-lis of your teeth.

## NEWBIES

Driving for the first time in months, we're out
in cream air, old roads, lobbed estates seeping
by the rim of each roundabout –
the weedy local bypass, a single show house empty.

We keep our moss-rimmed windows down
to trap the disembodied birdsong, our foreign news
for miles. Let's imagine we are far, far from death,
from the declivities and grey roses of death

and rushing by grunting farm compactors,
a sweet smell of pig shit, racing silent wheat.
We learn to treasure mulch sheets and beets,
our thighs sticking to the vinyl seats like this.

And debating some sort of graceless future,
one we never hope to drive to, with blind maps
prepared to capture us like town wreckage,
hoping to escape from our age as age envelops us.

# NCP

Just a few floors above the diesel Dominators
and the soot-chased low frame of the bus station,
there are the rippled floors of foxed concrete,
the white combs and cross-hatching of the parking lots.

Louvred doors hide the singing generators
and each floor imitates the other in structure and support –
a gorgeous, airy absence of outlook.
There's falling light and sodium-lit panels like metallic saints

marking each denomination of the perilous ascent.
Then the steel casings and digital focus of the ticket machines
proving we rest in the glories of a temporal gullet.
The cast, permanent, skeletal fusion

and urine-coated stairwell of this habitat.
Its polka dots of chewing gum on the fetid surface
of the polished cement. And I can see the burst vesicles
in its surface; its smooth, pock-marked, ice-cold skin.

There are rent boys in wind-cheaters beatified
on shadowy gantries near the grey velour of what little paint work.
The trembling, immoderate vistas of darkened windows
where security lights admit each faceless nineteenth

century, civic office with golden apostolic light.
Small haloes and gauzes where the late evening noise
collates the tempestuous backwash of traffic.
I can see only departures between buildings, from mall to mall,

the quaking brilliance and shift of crowds.
The break up and solitary journeys here, past the hammered

steel of the broken lift doors, the soiled corners
beyond the hooked-up, echoey chassis

of the temple. These chauffeured pillars
of concrete boxing our damaged, rigid lung,
where the stark numerals of each level wrench and remind.
An unprotected, solid stench, which coaxes others

buried with bags, to jostle children and climb
through the blind corridors to each codified gap.
It's barren like the stars, this cage of air, definite and emptying.
Like the hostel of something carnal and immanent.

## THE CUPBOARD

Somewhere in my moon mind
stuck in the back of an old stair cupboard
I find the things I cannot know –
dusts from June a hundred years ago,

green wires and bare wires and
tufty crochets of spider webs,
one glove, worse for wear, a box of fuses,
things everybody loses.

And in the warm must and tatters
forgotten coats from twenty winters back,
a grey cricket ball, a single laceless shoe,
a hardened tube of glue.

I shan't throw anything away, gathering
what's useless here forever, to hint at something
that mattered once when the swallows came
and your death had not happened.

## THE MAESTRO

I reach your bath chair, berthed upon the patio.
It is two o'clock forever, with chickens and parrots.
I step into pink shade dressed as a bridal nurse
clutching a paring knife. A blind dog dreams.
You raise a hand and lift up Holofernes
ready to be stripped of peel. I place an apple slice
in your mouth. Who will save you from this tryst?
Soon we shall have news of the matinee, Jacopo
and Alessio, wide-hipped, all smiles, fresh from the opera –
frock-coated patrons reporting your desire. Naturally,
the rehearsal was a triumph, the mezzo danced
into a frugal coffin mistaking it for her lover's bed,
the rustic chorus roared out, *contra mundum*,
at each ancient joke. They say you are the maestro
of the demitasse, the saviour of farce. Ciao, sweet Lord.
New shadows of conifers bleed across gravel,
and end up pointing fingers at your poor forgotten feet.

## THE ESTABLISHMENT OF THE SCENE

Your wretched car wreck by the South Gate steams
under monstrous azaleas from which
footprints trail over lawn frost and light spills
from that electric bedroom, reaching us.

Mrs Soames in her torn nightdress singing
folk songs to a lost tattered child stands near
and a smooth cascade of fog reaches up
to the crepuscular smashed-in glasshouse.

Glades of buried roses, low sandstone walls,
(wheels of your upturned Austin spinning still).
Matching swans chalked out on a bleeding lake
with statues of Janus and Diana.

Wisteria-covered Georgian frontage
tormented with fragrances of bad earth.
We reach the huge door, its handle plunges
and we enter old particular hells.

Numinous, timber-lined hall with gurning
portraits in reeves and one line of black boots.
We yearn for each other noticing bloodsmeared
faces for the first time since the death.

Soon, flashbacks kill our pyjama moment,
and we leap into faceless gilt mirrors
owning mad amounts of luggage, old fears,
smart jazz squeals under the stylus, we dance.

Everything becomes perpetual white.
A visitor solves the door to your room
and explodes his facial cavity now.
Our end is your beginning. Titles. Snow.

## EMBOUCHURE

Well, we're lucky it's still here, just
name the last street, Chet. It's sweet
to blow another year out, the faint bloom
forever on a twilight club, cutting the mirror,
but our taxi noses by to tease

and take the love road under no one's light,
a rose neighbourhood that swells for now
in brushes and sweet bass,
the chords that fill your teeth,

don't run the notes to live them,
kiss those easy nights on the soft canals,
a cutesy sheen the maps bring home:
white organza, slacks and shirt,
a leap of notes sucked in to be clean
and O those gorgeous awful stars.

## A MANCHESTER TALE

Coke smoke and sulphur light and dim hoof taps.
Green air that spells out spiced slave tobacco
in echoes on Dantzic Street.

Pigs in a yard and cinders and giddy stars and you, my love.
Nothing one could braise or feed the young but
horse meat.

A queue of shadows and a murder in that yellow rain
and no shoes in the yard and the kids on fire so long ago
in Angel Meadow.

I could fetch you thrills, a score of Christmas teeth,
soot you could lose a hearse in, rags and bills,
my foot in the door, singing of Castlebar, my love.

## COW PARSLEY

*for Rory Waterman*


That you can't easily move through while wet May dies,
vulgar and disconsolate and heavy scented:
ghost fringe of unadopted lanes,
nova of hedgerows.

And here you are again so common and abundant
enjoying the florid shade. You fill it briefly
which tells us all of being young, if you can remember
the flurry, the hustle,

all that sweet showiness we go through while May dies
and another season crams its heat
into the centre of you, grown so tall,
then suddenly it is over.

## SCARP

As and when we leer through town tomorrow
the last of the bad men will fry on the bypass
struggling past the city centre with its rhinestoned busker.
Some sort of dawn will send its tears of waste over any
Google map that could pin us there, we shan't be found
below the eighty-foot slag barrow:
a memorial to one million lungs, a place
landscaped like it could send out a moral outcome
to the districts of laths and lit up spars and gantries.

All day long, spitting crowds look at nothing,
I ask you, whom do the coal saints pray for?
How many children should be wired in rooms or beaten flat?
How many marriages licked into walls like that?
Who picks up each second hand peacoat to pound out
a dead song six storeys down in the glory hole,
coveting nothing beyond last year's gas bill or
posters for a life of scars? Dip the clutch, Ruthie,
let's push on through, no one needs a life like this.

# BEGINNINGS

Sea lunge. The slip-feed. The wash dragged so far
from its brine skin to breathe light over reeds.
Something leaking iodine. A large pier.
High-density polyethylene. Sheds,
yes, filled with cut coils of drying Nuflex.
The storm surge nightwear. A promenade's bins.
Something lost and screaming where lands relax
into the boulder ridge, where gabions
twist their cold stanzas. Dawn's unlost loves
curtained in sweeping hail. The slowest east.
Everything counting and counted that shoves
from grey acres into one venal feast.
The night's heart stoppages on a white deck.
The gull cloud on our fresh red wake.

## THINGS THAT I CAN NEVER TEACH YOU

1.

On the naked north side of nubby elms
you step among gravestones and know the breeze
and see outside this wall borderless fields dip
to an unseen Atlantic shoreline and
there is a moss greener than her eyes.

2.

When you bend and blow carefully at the flame
its heat lifts yesterday's ash a little
but all the gods will not travel to your heart,
for their coat is the coldest to wear, their love
is rinsing absence.

3.

Eventually, they all leave for the gaunt city
and the next frost hunts the fox lanes bringing up
one hand after another to the store of your mind.
There will be a small sound, footsteps on gravel,
that you must let into you and keep.

4.

One palmful of earth, with its rusty linen smell
and rotten story is all that fills the journey for you.
Life is peril and demesne. You have your taut dawn
without a country to wince at, pegging out
blouse after slapping blouse on a damp rope.

## THE START OF IT

But there will come a time, you'll surely know it,
in a restaurant, or the traffic's slur and rapture
on a ringing bridge, perhaps, or singing on a green hill.
It may be early autumn with a spur of geese
above you on a wet lane, with all the lights coming on –
you'll be distracted, too – but there will come a time
and you will know your own time passing.
Nothing too dramatic, it's not a scare you'll have,
but something abstract stiffens in the grace of it,
and there will be a sense of wine twisting from the lip
of an ewer, or of one decaying wind before a curtain of rain.
And you'll see the formal shape you make in time,
the here and there of sweet things and bitter things
we all carry silently – and that will be the start of it.

## THE LEGACY

You use your father's
winter paring knife
to ease it free,
all strange paper weather
with none of the weight
a child expects of it

and when you send it down,
studiously gentle
from high, bolted,
cobwebbed beams
into my hands
like this, it is

sad and gorgeously dented,
a featherweight haul
the wasps have left
to drone in apple acres
elsewhere darkening
with sweet ruin now.

## ACKNOWLEDGEMENTS

Thank you to Tony and Angela at Arc, for starting me on my journey as a writer over twenty years ago, and for allowing me to continue it in these pages. My last collection was titled *The Departure*, this book feels more like an arrival.

I would like to thank the editors of the following magazines, where some of these poems first appeared: *Ambit, Bad Lilies, Fenland Poetry Journal, Ink Sweat & Tears, The London Magazine, The Moth, PN Review* and *Shearsman Magazine*.

Thank you to Moniza Alvi, Niall Campbell, John Kinsella and Anne Rouse for their generous comments on the poems. I'm grateful to James Sutherland-Smith for his critical eye and generosity.

Special thanks to Michael Symmons Roberts for reading my Ranworth poem.

I owe a debt to the poets at the Butchery Workshop in Norwich – to Helen and Martin, who run that space, and to Andrea, Andrew, Esther, Joanna, Jon and Tiffany.

Thanks to Neil Campbell for his advice when the well ran dry, and to Martin Malone who helped me to continue writing in new directions and, indeed, into my next collection.

My gratitude to Gerard Beirne whose online friendship gave me confidence to push on during the pandemic.

Thanks to Steven Fowler for inviting me to collaborate with Richard Lambert as part of the European Poetry Night in 2017, where 'The Bittern' was first performed.

Huge thanks to the tireless Florrie Crass and Home Stage Poetry, to Elisabeth Sennitt Clough and the team at Poetry in Aldeburgh, to the team at the Blakeney Harbour Room's Folk, Poetry and Beer Festival, to Richard Skinner and the organisers of the Margate Bookie and, lastly, to Gale Burns and the team at The Shuffle, where some of these poems were first performed.

My love to Jennifer, for over thirty years of support on just about every front imaginable – and to our children, who have to put up with me.

And thanks to you, for reading the poems.

## BIOGRAPHICAL NOTE

CHRIS EMERY was born in Manchester in 1963. He is a director of Salt, an independent trade publisher, and is the former Director of Operations and Director of Development for The Shrine of Our Lady of Walsingham in North Norfolk.

He has published three collections of poetry, a writer's guide, an anthology of art and poems, and edited selections of Emily Brontë, Keats and Rossetti.

.